UDAAN

A graphic glimpse through the life of Praful Patel.

यद्यदाचरति श्रेष्ठस्तत्तदेवेतरो जनः ।
स यत्प्रमाणं कुरुते लोकस्तदनुवर्तते ॥

WHICHEVER AND HOWEVER A GREAT PERSONALITY CONDUCTS HIMSELF COMMON MEN DO ALSO; WHATEVER HE ACCEPTS AS AUTHORITY THAT AND THAT ALONE CERTAINLY ALL THE WORLD WILL FOLLOW.

BHAGAVAD GITA CHAPTER 3 / 21

Dedicated to the late Manoharbhai Patel,
father and role model of Shri Praful Patel

PRESENTED BY
MUKESH GANDHI
19A Dhiraj Apt., Peddar Road
Mumbai - 400 026, India
gandhimg51@gmail.com
M: 98201 40165

- - - -

Published and distributed by
Roli Books
M-75, Greater Kailash II Market
New Delhi-110 048, India
Phone: ++91-11-4068 2000
E-mail: info@rolibooks.com
Website: www.rolibooks.com

- - - -

ISBN: 978-93-5194-194-1

- - - -

First edition 2017

- - - -

DESIGNER
Sandip Dixit

- - - -

WRITER
Timmy Verghese

- - - -

PRINTED BY
JAK Printers Pvt. Ltd.
www.jakprinters.com

- - - -

A sneak peak.

Having been closely acquainted with Prafulbhai since the last 20 years, I've always looked up to him, not just as a politician, but as a selfless human being who sees tremendous joy in the joy of others.

It has been more than six years since I first had this thought of creating this book. When I first excitedly told him, he dismissed it almost immediately. "I don't believe in all this show shaa", he said. But after a lot of coaxing, he finally relented– not to a biography, but a pictographic compilation.

Giving India more than 60 world-class airports, initiating numerous social educational institutions, giving a fillip to governance, contributing to the sports sector. enhancing art and culture. These are just a few of the things that Prafulbhai was passionately involved in over the years.

He's one who doesn't make empty promises. But what he talks about, he makes sure it sees the light of day. For example, it was during his tenure as Aviation Minister that India's middle class actually started flying.

Through all the achievements and accolades, Prafulbhai remains grounded. Having lost his father at the tender age of 13, he's what you could define clearly as a self-made man. On one hand he is extremely humble and easygoing, yet on the other, absolutely strict and rigid about his principles. And that's what, I think, leaves all those who interact with him, in total awe.

As a team, it took us five years to gather and sort the pictures to bring this book together. I'm thankful to all those who helped along the way. And my sincere apologies to many whose photographs we might have missed out.

To Praful Patel, a leader, a mentor, a friend, I present this pictographic compilation, Udaan.

Mukesh Gandhi

Mukesh Gandhi

The Sky isn't the Limit

Praful Manoharbhai Patel is one of the modern visionaries of our country. Hailing from the Gondia district of Maharashtra, he was first elected as the Municipal Council President of Gondia in 1985. Further, he was elected to the Lok Sabha in 1991. Since then he has till date been continuously elected to Parliament, four times to the Lok Sabha and twice to the Rajya Sabha. In 2004, he took over as the Minister for Civil Aviation. His next role made him the Minister of Heavy Industries and Public Enterprises. All this apart, Mr. Patel spends most of his time following his religion – serving society. His various social activities that have lovingly been imbibed into him by his father stay on to touch millions of chords in many a heart time and again.

This book is just a humble pictographic compilation, and a tribute to the illustrious journey of Praful Patel.

Reflections

The journey begins.

Some stories are worth recording. And the life and times of the Patel family is one such. Driven by poverty, Manoharbhai Patel, a young boy from Nadiad, Gujarat left his home in search of a way to fend for his family. He reached Jabalpur where he found a job as a truck loader and then as a cycle salesman. Soon he left Jabalpur and travelled around Central India doing odd jobs. Finally, as fate had it, he ended up in Gondia, to work with his uncle who then owned a tobacco shop in the area.

Over time, he worked closely with his uncle and helped him set up a beedi business. To say this turned out successful would be an understatement. Manoharbhai soon rose not only in fortune, but in respect too, across the communities of the region. Since he did not have access to formal education in his childhood, Manoharbhai's first wish was to bring education to the needy. At that time, in the entire 200 kms stretch of Gondia & Bhandara districts with a population of 20 lakhs, there was only one High School.To suffice this need, he set up the Gondia Education Society. And thus began the first of many institutions that would later come to be a colossus with 60 institutions, 1,10,000 students and 5000 teachers and employees.

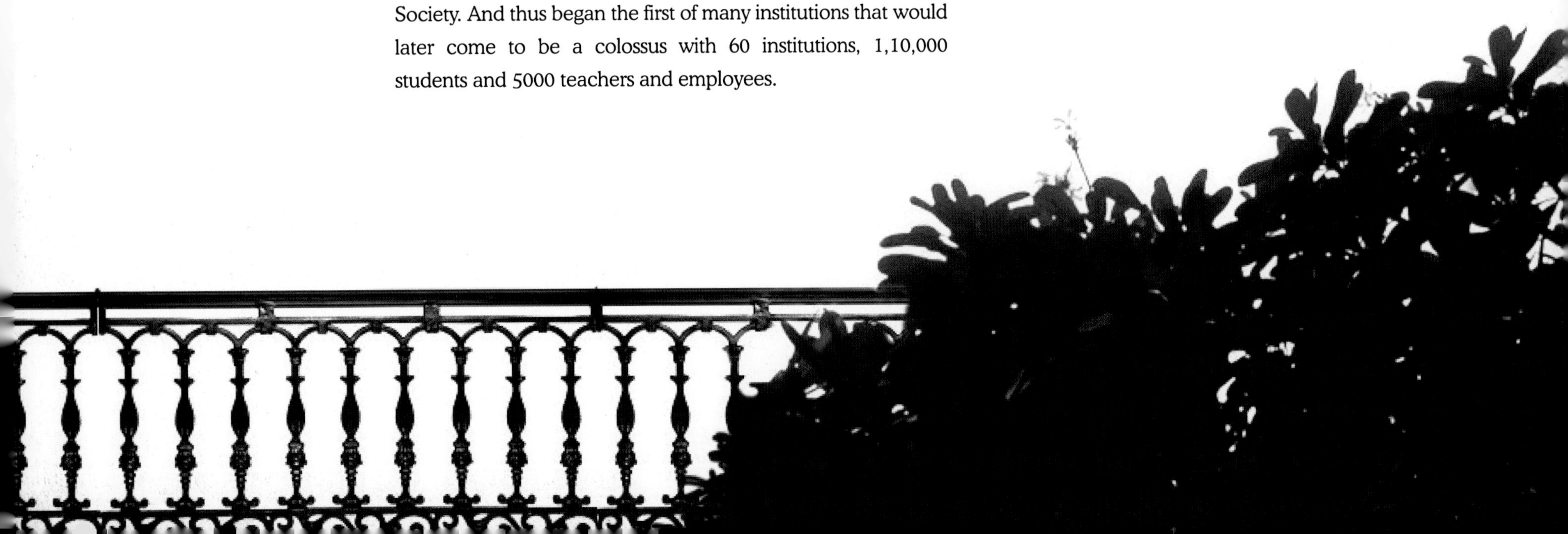

The philanthropic journey of Manoharbhai Patel had begun. On the political front meanwhile he was elected as the Municipal President of Gondia, a post he held till his death 25 years later. He was a legislator in the assembly of erstwhile Central Provinces and Berar and then a member of the Legislative Assembly of Maharashtra after its formation in 1960. Manoharbhai was one amongst the powerful triumvirate with Y.B. Chavan and V.P. Naik. Though he was President of the Congress Party, he chose not to enter the government, which would have come to him naturally.

Manoharbhai also played host in Gondia to many dignitaries like Mahatma Gandhi, Jawaharlal Nehru, Jayprakash Narayan and Indira Gandhi, to name a few.

Manoharbhai and Shantaben.

With political mentor Pandit Ravishankar Shukla (Chief Minister of Central Provinces and Berar)

With close friends V. P. Naik (Chief Minister of Maharashtra) and Y. B. Chavan (Defence Minsiter of India)

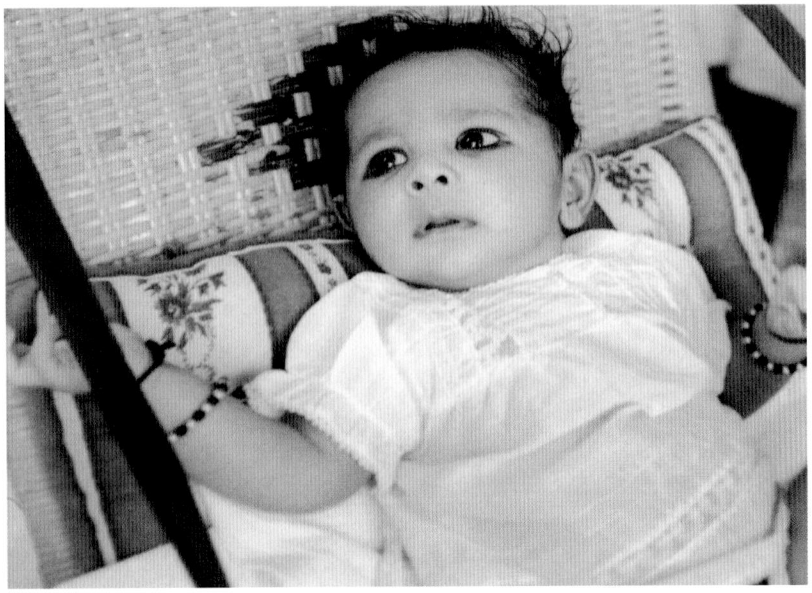

The Birth of Praful

On February 17, 1957, at Park Nursing home in Kolkota, Shantaben gave birth to Praful Patel. An only child, his birth was a cause of immense celebration. Though he had a privileged childhood, one of the first lessons his father taught him was to never let his upbringing go to his head.

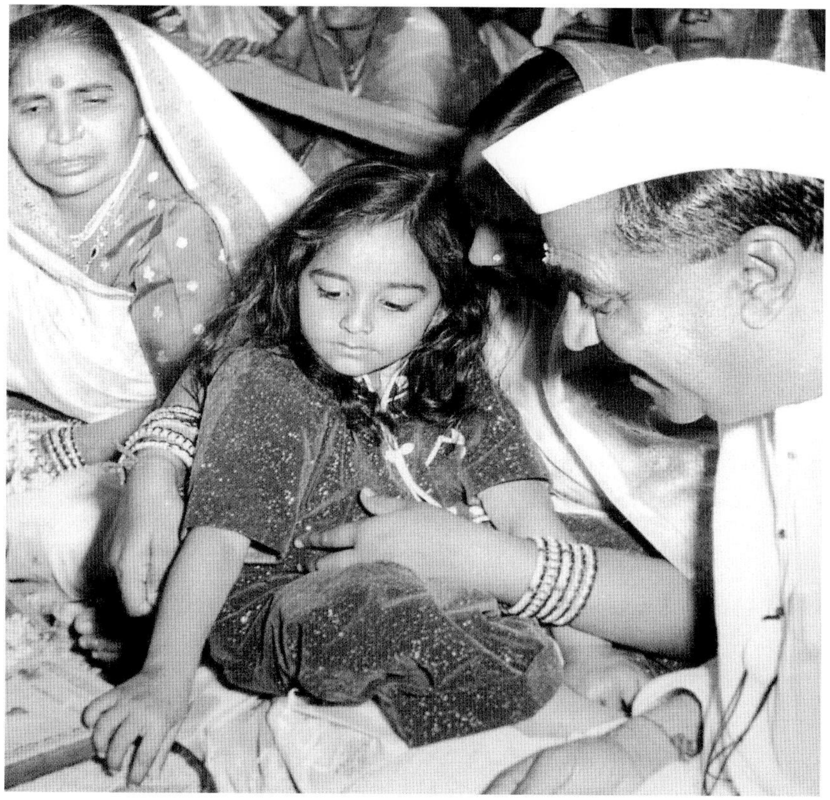

Early years.

With friends in Gondia.

Growing up

The years that followed laid the foundation for the philosophy and beliefs that Praful Patel is made of today. He was a charismatic and socially loved young man who had natural leadership qualities from his childhood itself.

Manoharbhai made it a point that Praful interacted and was a part of as many of his important meetings as possible. And this proved to be a great training ground for this young boy who would then go on to take over many important roles.

When he was four, he was sent to Mumbai to get a quality education, something that Manoharbhai was deprived of.

With international consultants, reviewing a project site in Mumbai, now known as Ceejay House.

One Era Ends

On August 17, 1970, when Praful was just 13, Manoharbhai breathed his last. His funeral, as older inhabitants of Gondia still remember was one of the biggest the country had ever seen at that time. People across the nation came by to pay homage to a man who touched their lives in ways much more than just political. The people of Gondia, even four decades after his death, are still in awe of this amazing leader who uplifted them in many ways.

Several initiatives that Manoharbhai began are now looked after by the Patel family. The institutions have students pursuing disciplines ranging from Arts, Commerce, Engineering, Law and Pharmacy to Information Technology and Computer Sciences. Through all these educational and charitable endeavors, the eternal flame of Manoharbhai's rich legacy stay alive and burning bright, to this day.

Manoharbhai's body being brought from Mumbai to Gondia.

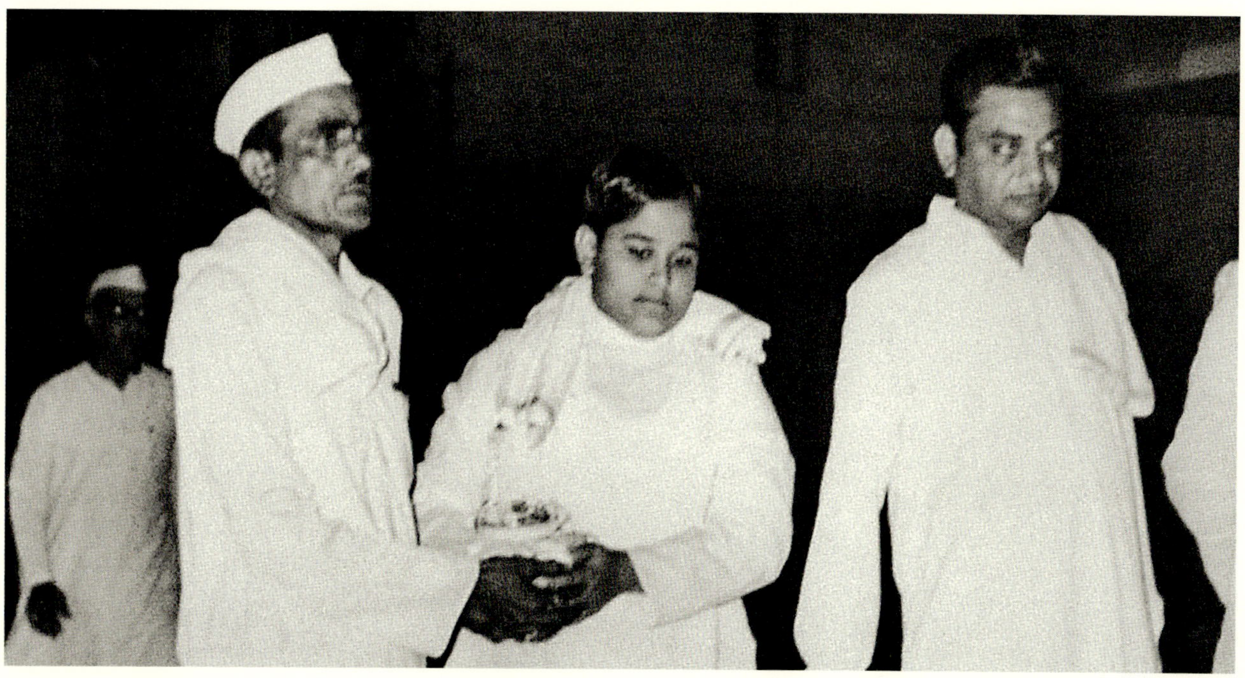

Beginning the last rites.

A funeral procession like never before, for a man who touched lives every waking moment.

A New Era Begins

At a very tender age, Praful Patel was handed the reins of his father's legacy. He had to take on the responsibility of looking after the family business and also carry on the social work that Manoharbhai had lovingly started. He alternated between his studies at Mumbai's Campion School and Sydenham College with his work in Gondia.

As the years passed, Praful on his young shoulders dedicatedly carried forward the work that Manoharbhai had started off. The journey that began then came a long way.

Visionaries build what dreamers imagine, they say. And the pages that follow justify this in every way.

You meet thousands of people and none of them really touch you, and then you meet one person and your life is changed forever.

Praful and Varsha.

The Better Half

At the age of 21, Praful met Varsha for the first time at a family function at Nadiad, Gujarat. Though a formal proposal came much later, it was love at first sight. She was pursuing her Bachelors Degree in Anand at that time. Praful found in her an extension of his personality and a partner in the great vision he fostered for a change in society. In 1977, they were married in a grand ceremony in Nadiad.

Varsha's humility and simplicity remain just the same to this day. Though a soft spoken home-maker, she is a strong willed support and a pillar of inspiration behind the man that Praful Patel is today.

A better half, truly.

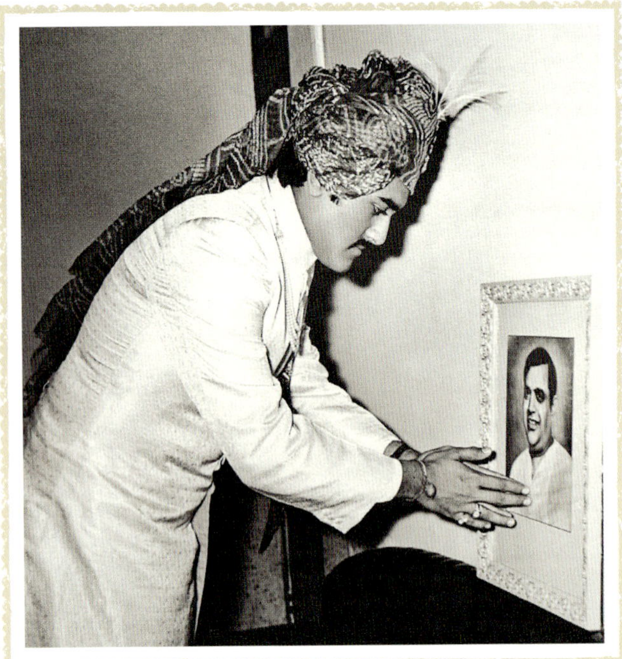

The wedding ceremony in Nadiad.

The family grew... Daughters Avni, Niyati, Poorna & Son Prajay.

Foray into Public Life

Growing up witnessing Manoharbhai's deep involvement with people, it was only natural that Praful was soon thrown into social and public life. Not that he complained ever. Praful's involvement with people and the flair with which he conducted his interactions saw him take up different responsibilities and roles over the years.

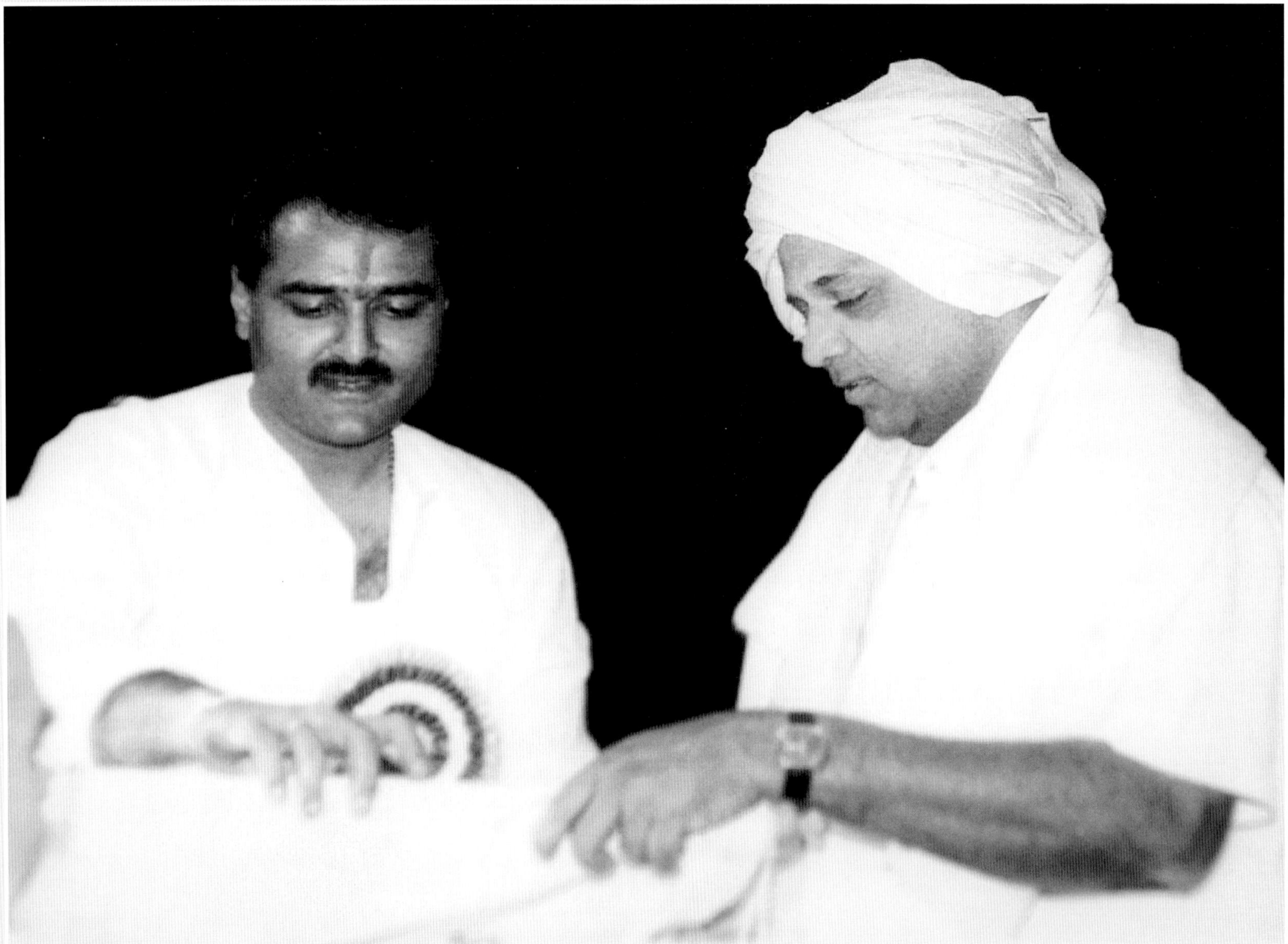

Early days with mentor Sharad Pawar.

After his victory as President of Municipal Council, Gondia.

Bhatia

At a rally in Gondia.

कार्यालय नगर परिषद, गोंदिया

लोककर्म विषय समिती १९८७-८८

बाएं से दाएं बैठे हुए श्री हरिदास मेश्राम, श्री सुंदरलाल यादव, श्री दामोदर अग्रवाल, (उपाध्यक्ष) श्री प्रफुल्लभाई पटेल, (अध्यक्ष) श्री भगत ठकरानी, (सभापति) श्री ओंकारलाल अग्रवाल, श्री अजीतकुमार जैन, श्री सतीश राऊत, श्रीमती सुशीलाबाई उके, श्री गोविंद आस्वानी, श्री दाजीबा मानापूरे, श्री भोलाजी फुंडे, एड. विनोदकुमार जानी, श्री लक्ष्मनजी बिसेन, श्री रमेश ठवरे, पीछे खडे है बाँए से श्री धुले (प्लानिंग क्लर्क) श्री रमन रमादे (प्रभारी क्लर्क), श्री आत्माराम, व अन्य चपरासी, श्री रामटेककर (ओव्हरसियर)।

Inspecting a flood affected area with close confidante Rajendra Jain.

Intertacing with villagers during his 400 km walk at Farmers Rally.

Ushering in new trains to his constituency.

78820/78819 गोंदिया–बल्लारशाह–गोंदिया
78820/78819 GONDIA-BALLARSHAH-GONDIA
दपूम
SEC

दक्षिण पूर्व रेलवे
का उद्घाटन

Taking a site review of an irrigation project under construction.

An election rally in Surat, Gujarat.

An election rally in Gondia, Maharashtra.

Victory procession after the Look Sabha elections.

महाप्रज्ञा बुध्द विहार लोकार्पण
भीम

At a Buddhist gathering.

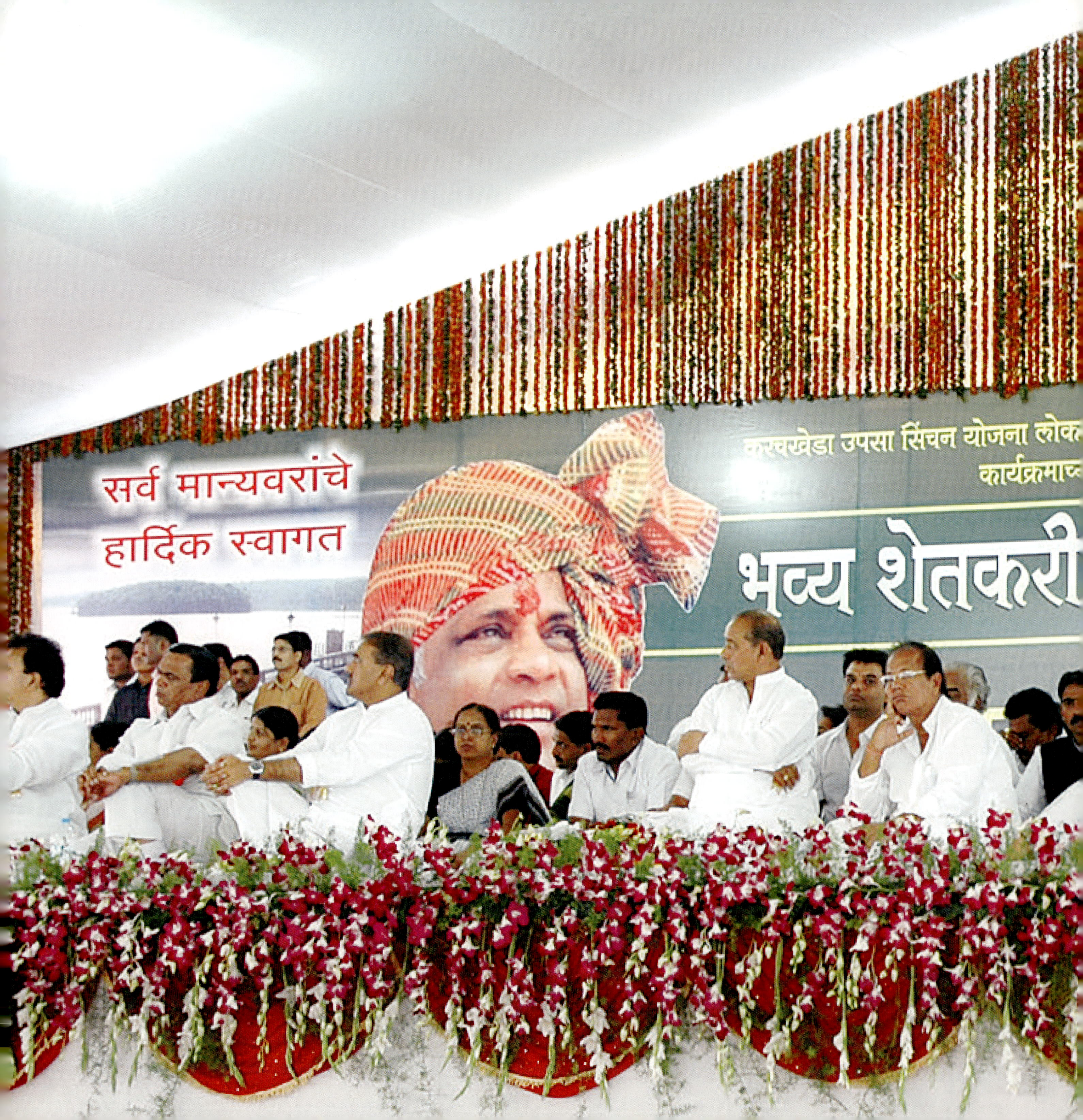
सर्व मान्यवरांचे
हार्दिक स्वागत
भव्य शेतकरी

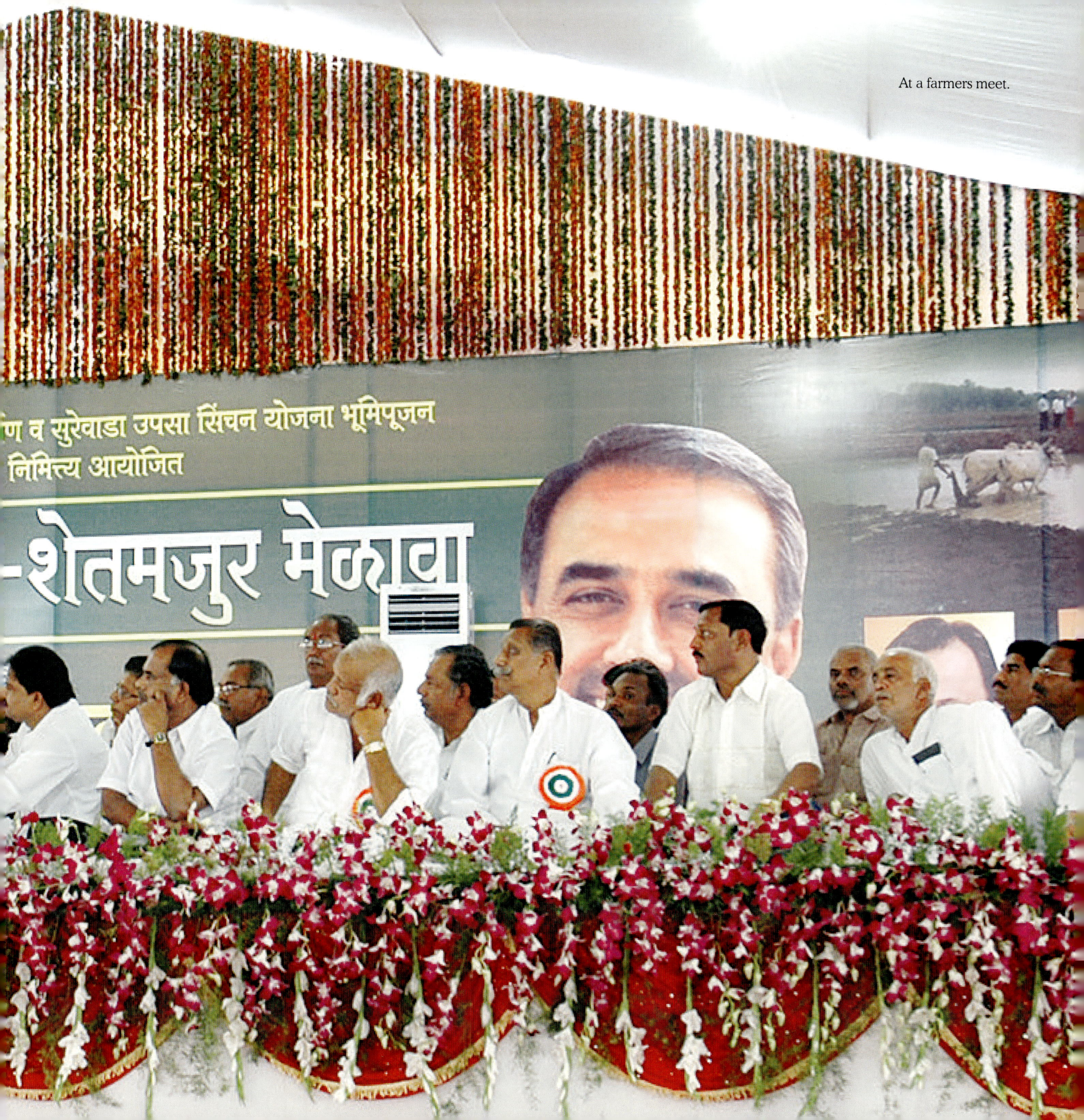

At a farmers meet.

A workshop on inland fisheries.

Promoting sugarcane farming and sugar factories.

Unveiling a new statue.

Unveiling the statue of Manoharbhai Patel in Gondia.

With Anil Deshmukh, Venugopal Dhoot, Mukesh Ambani, Murli Deora, Digvijay Singh, Vilasrao Deshmukh, Bhairon Singh Shekhawat, Sharad Pawar, Vijay Mallya, Yashodhara Raje Scindia, Hariharbhai Patel, Gopal Agarwal and other guests.

Addressing villagers in his constituency.

At an election meeting.

Release function of a commemorative stamp of Manoharbhai Patel by dignitaries.

जयंती
दिवस
फरवरी २०
भारत
INDIA
मा. प्रफुल पटेल

At an annual function on his father's birth anniversary, to felicitate young students.

स्व. मनोहरभाई पटेल
पदक वितरण समारोह
जयंती
दिवस
१ फरवरी २०१३

At NCP Party Women's rally with Shri. Sharad Pawar & Smt. Supriya Sule.

With Amar Singh, Sharad Pawar, Prime Minister Chandrashekhar and Sonia Gandhi.

With Prime Minister H. D. Deve Gowda.

With Prime Minister Narasimha Rao and Sharad Pawar.

With Prime Minister Shri. Narendra Modi.

At the launch of the Piaggio plant in Baramati.

With Shivsena President Shri. Uddhav Thackeray.

With Amitabh Bachchan, Shekhar Gupta, Sunil Mittal, Dr. Naresh Trehan & Sunil Munjal at an award function.

With Shri. Subhash Chandra handing over the first copy of DNA Newspaper to Prime Minister Dr. Manmohan Singh

President of India Pranab Mukharjee, Vice President of India M. Hamid Ansari, Prime Minister of India Narendra Modi, NCP Chief Sharad Pawar, former Prim
Bihar Chief Minister Nitish Kumar, Union Minister M. Venkaiah Naidu, Rajsthan Chief Minister Vasundhara Raje, Maharashtra Chief Minister Devendra Fadnavis,Lo
Former Minister Ghulam Nahi Azad, Union Finance minister Arun Jaitley, Lok Sabha M

Minister Manmohan Singh, Pratibha Pawar, Congress President Sonia Gandhi,CPI(M) General Secretary Sitaram Yechury, RJD President Lalu Prasad Yadav, abha Speaker of India Sumitra Mahajan, Former Minister Farooq Abdullah, Samajwadi Party Chief Mulayam Singh Yadav, Congress Vice President Rahul Gandhi, . K. Advani, Punjab Chief Minister Prakash Singh Badal, Supriya Sule & Praful Patel.

Minister for Civil Aviation

Flagging off a new Air India flight.

Overseeing the construction of modern airports across the country in a time-bound manner.

DELHI
GMR
Canyon from Departure Level

Sharing development plans with Sonia Gandhi.

an A-380

At an Air India Funetion

With officials of United States Federal Aviation Authority

Inauguration of T3, Delhi.

At the inauguration ceremony of Istanbul Airport.

In the cockpit of a new Air India aircraft.

With the Prime Minister Manmohan Singh on the arrival of Air India's brand new fleet.

RAJIV GAND
INTERNATIO
KINLEY

AIRPORT
KINLEY

Launching India's first air-show.

AIRBUS
A319 Delivery to AIR INDIA

शिलान्यास समारोह

With Chief Minister Narendra Modi at the Foundation stone laying ceremony of Ahmedabad International Airport.

प्राधिकरण
हवाई अड्डा, नागपुर
भारत रत्न डा. बी आर
प्रतिमा का
टर्मिनल भवन का

At the inauguration of the new terminal and installation of the statue of Dr. Babasaheb Ambedkar at Nagpur Airport.

International Airport
Ground
Praful Patel

Arrival canopy at the International Terminal, Mumbai.

Ground breaking ceremony of the New International Terminal of Mumbai Airport.

Gondia Airport.

A function at the National Flying School in Gondia with Kapil Sibal, Madhur Bhandarkar.

TH FEBRUARY, 2010

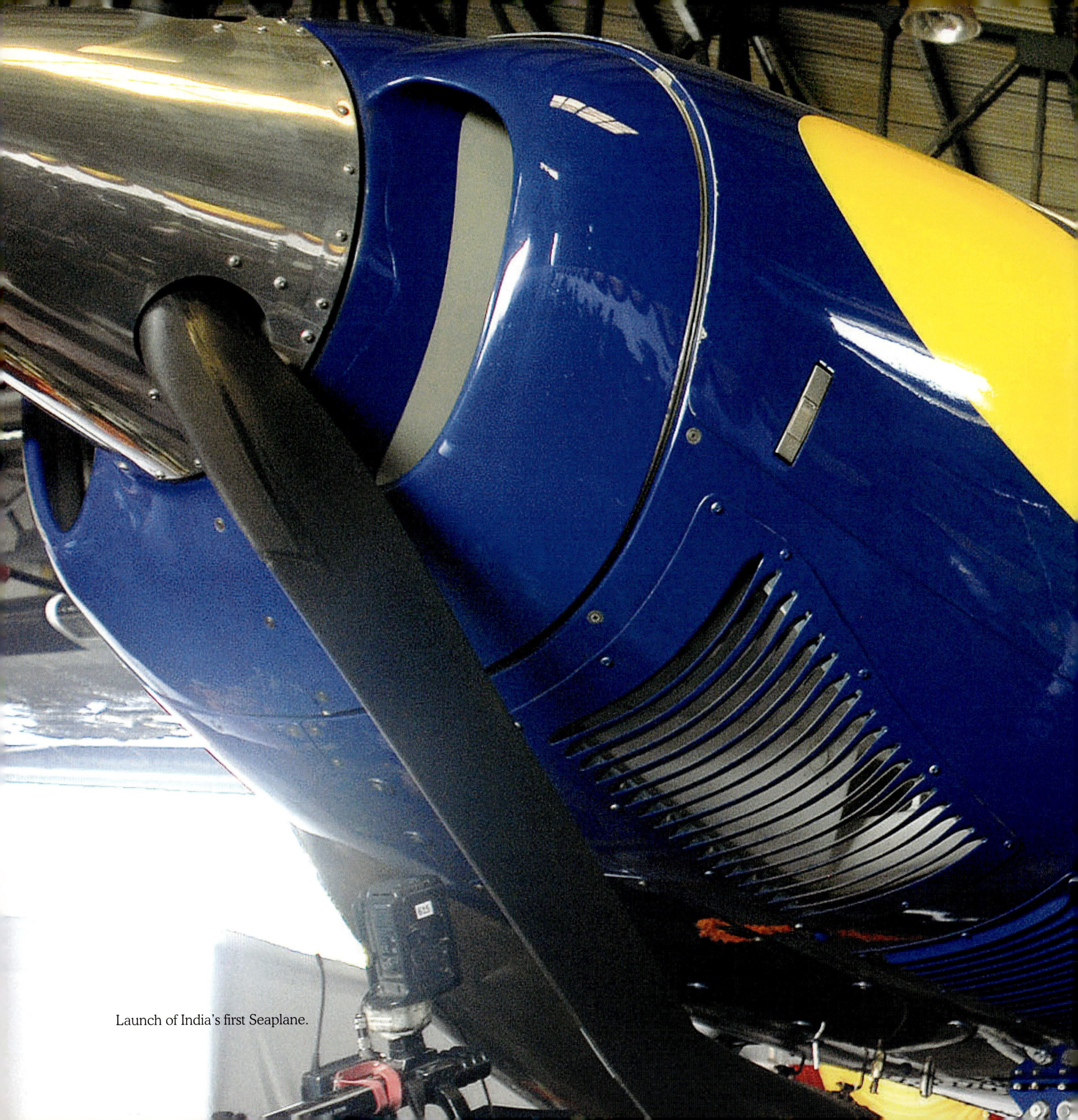

Launch of India's first Seaplane.

Marylyn

In 2004, Praful Patel took over as the Minister for Civil Aviation.

Liberal skies, more connectivity, increased competition, low cost airlines, led to more choice, cheaper fares and better facilities for passengers. For the first time a common man could fulfill his dream to fly. India soon became the eighth largest aviation market in the world and will become the third largest by 2025.

Our old airports were his priority. In a short span of five years more than 60 airports across the country were reconstructed to the best of global standards. Air traffic systems were modernized and India became only the fourth country to have its own satellite for Air Navigation and Communication Systems.

Truly a new era was ushered in.
A revolution in the skies had begun.

Chatrapati Shivaji International Airport, Mumbai.

T3, Indira Gandhi International Airport, New Delhi.

TERMINAL3
टर्मिनल 3
आगमन ARRIVALS
प्रीमियम
Premium
टैक्सी
Taxi
आगमन
कारें
Cars

T3, Indira Gandhi International Airport, New Delhi.

Indore Airport

Interior view of Bhopal Airport.

Interior view of Udaipur Airport.

Interior view of Srinagar International Airport.

ATC Tower, Mumbai

Netaji Subhash Chandra Bose International Airport, Kolkata.

Bengaluru International Airport

Dibrugarh Airport

Tirupati Airport

RAJIV GANDHI INTERNATIONAL AIR

Rajiv Gandhi International Airport, Hyderabad.

Interior view of Srinagar International Airport.

Aurangabad Airport

Ahmedabad Airport.

Chennai International Airport

Dehradun Airport

Jaipur Airport

Surat Airport

Minister of Heavy Industries & Public Enterprises

The massive 3300 MW Adani Power Project at Gondia.

At a Public Sector Day function with President Pratibha Patil.

Public Sector day awards ceremony with President Pranab Mukherjee.

With the German Minister of Transport and the Ambassador of Germany.

Foundation laying of BHEL Plant in Bhandara Constituency

A gathering of all the heads of Public Sector Maharatna and Navratna companies.

Overseeing the construction of New Industries and Power Projects.

India's first Hybrid and Electric Vehicles.

At a book release with the governor of Maharashtra and Mukesh Ambani

Looking at the future of the automobile.

At an award function with Anand Mahindra

With US President Barrack Obama and first-lady Michelle Obama.

With U.S. Secretary of Transportation Norman Mineta.

With President Francois Hollande & Ambassador Richier of France.

In conversation with US President Bill Clinton.

With Hillary Clinton.

With the royal family of Qatar.

With President of Pakistan Pervez Musharraf.

Honorary Doctorate from Leeds Metropolitan University for outstanding contribution to Nation Building.

President of the
All India Football Federation.

The Sports Enthusiast

1994 FIFA World Cup USA
1998 FIFA World Cup France
Tricolore

With (L to R) John Abraham, Sachin Tendulkar, Ranbir Kapoor, Abhishek Bachhan, Neeta Ambani & Varun Dhavan.

With Shaikh Salman bin Ebrahim Al Khalifa, President, Asian Football Confederation
& Smt. Nita Ambani, Founder Chairperson, Football Sports Developement

With FIFA President Sepp Blatter

CHAM

PIONS

At a festival match in Bhandara with Indian Cricket Captain M. S. Dhoni and others.

With Sachin Tendulkar and Vijay Darda.

Heart & Soul

At a Buddha Vihar in Bhandara.

Paying tribute to Bhagwan Birsa Munda at a tribal rally.

With Sharad Pawar and Prithviraj Chavan at an Iftaar function in Haj house, Mumbai.

Praying at Shiva Mandir.

Praying at Hanuman Mandir.

At Santram Mandir, Nadiad, Gujarat.

मा.ना.श्री प्रफुल पटेल यांच्या प्रयत्नातून निर्धारित वेळेपूर्वीच साकार
नॅचरल ग्रोवर्स प्रायवेट लि. लाखांदूर
द्वारा संचालित लाखांदुर येथील अत्याधुनिक साखर कारखान्याचा
चाचणी गाळप शुभारंभ

At a function for the handicapped.

One of the institutions of Gondia Education Society, a temple of learning for 1,10,000 students.

March-past at Sainik School, Gondia

A department of the Manoharbhai Patel College of Engineering.

National Flying Training Institute, Gondia.

One of the several Mass Wedding Ceremonies comprising all religions, conducted by the Manoharbhai Patel Foundation.

Family & Friends

Holidaying with the family at Maldives.

On holiday in Scotland.

Boating on Dal Lake, Srinagar.

At Amarnath with daughter.

LOOKS 26
FEELS 22
ACTS 12
THAT MAKES ME 60
VINTAGE
1957
AGED TO PERFECTION

With R.V. Deshpande, Radhaji and the entire family at Avni and Prashant's wedding.

With Utsav and Nilu Parekh at Niyati and Samarth's wedding.

With family patriarch Harshadbhai Dalal, partners Arvind Patel, Kiran Patel, Deepak Patel, Shailesh Patel and their families at a wedding function.

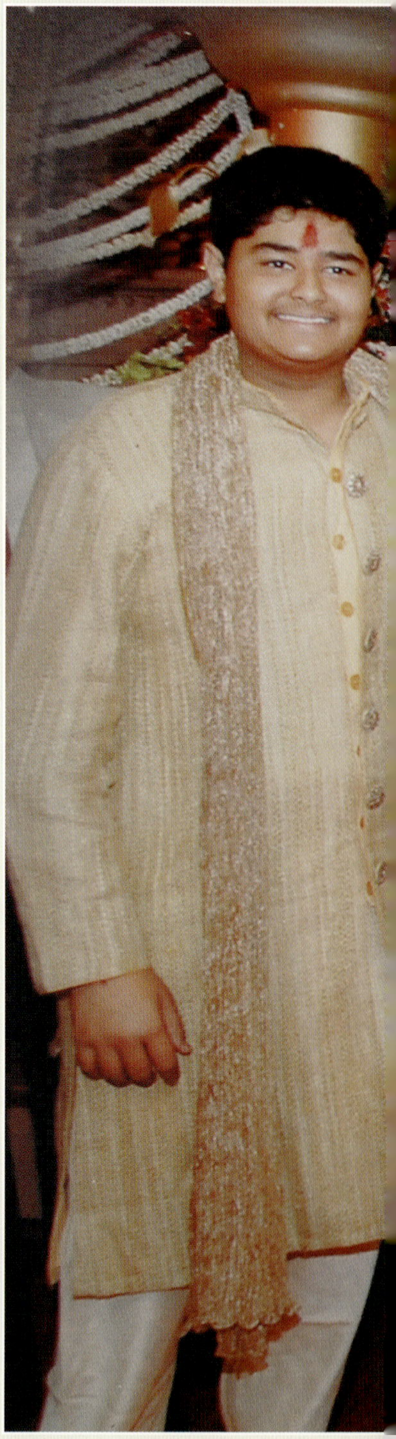

With Neeta & Mukesh Ambani during Avni & Prashant's wedding

With Salman Khan, Rajat Sharma & Suhel Seth at the Annual Award Function at Gondia.

With Mrs. & Mr. Sant Chatwal

With Amrish Patel.

With Shri. Mohanlal Mittal & Laxmi Mittal, at Niyati & Samarth's wedding

With Amitabh Bachchan, Amar Singh, Dilip Kumar & Saira Banu.

At a cultural function in Gondia with Saif Ali Khan, Shah Rukh Khan, Vijay Darda and Subhash Ghai.

With Dhirubhai Ambani at Gondia airport.

With Laxmi Mittal and S. P. Hinduja.

With Gautam Adani & Venugopal Dhoot.

Lighter moments

In Kazhakistan.

Holidaying in Bhutan

In Nagaland.

At the ET Cookout with Sunil Mittal

In Romania with his YPO forum friends :

L to R - Abhay Kanoria, Shishir Bajaj, Harsh Mariwala, Manu Mahtani, Praful Patel, Gurinder Singh, Sajjan Jindal, Rajan Mittal, Suketu Shah & Uday Kotak.

With Salman Khan at Niyati & Samarth's wedding

Having fun with his buddies, Surendra Ruia & TNV Ayyer.

at Home

With Son Prajay Patel

DANGER
VT-KSA

For tomorrow

The most important resource our country has is "us". I'm of the opinion that our vastness and diversity is our true strength. I wish we could take education and development to the far corners of our beautiful motherland, to each individual. That for me is true empowerment. I will do everything in my power to take this vision forward. So that together we can all walk into a tomorrow full of happiness and prosperity.

भारतीय कृत्रिम अंग निर्माण निगम, कानपुर
भारत सरकार का उपक्रम) द्वारा
Praful Patel